*Dedicated with love to my very patient nephew*
**Christopher Lee Congdon**

*With gratitude to*
**Margaret Cristiano** *for reuniting me with Alexandra Elizabeth,*
**John Rittell** *for his stalwart support,*
**Jean O'Neil** *for many gifts and*
**Anne McNamara** *for her courageous spirit*

# THE MOST IMPORTANT QUESTION

### H. CONSTANCE HILL
author and illustrator

❖ **Diamond Clear Vision** ❖

Copyright © 2011 by H. Constance Hill.

All rights reserved. No part of this book may be reproduced in any mechanical, photographic, or electronic process, or in the form of a phonographic recording; nor may it be stored in a retrieval system, transmitted, or otherwise be copied for public or private use, other than for "fair use" as brief quotations embodied in articles or reviews, without prior written permission of the publisher.

Cover Art and Interior Art © 2011 by H. Constance Hill
Book design by Pamela Marin-Kingsley, Far-Angel Design

Published by Diamond Clear Vision, an imprint of Illumination Arts LLC.
140 Adams Street, Quincy, MA 02169
United States of America

www.diamondclearvision.com
info@diamondclearvision.com

If you are unable to order this book from your local bookseller, you may order directly from the publisher.
Special quantity discounts for organizations are available.

**Library of Congress Control Number:  2011926856**

**ISBN: 978-0-9829225-6-9**

First Hardcover Edition

Printed by Shanghai Kangshi Printing Co. Ltd.

Once upon a time, not so long ago …

there lived a man named Albert Einstein. He was a scientist and very smart. Because he was so smart people called him Doctor Einstein. He liked to think about things. Thinking about one idea often led him to another, and then another. And another.

Doctor Einstein not only thought about things; he also asked questions. Then he enjoyed figuring out the answers. He figured out the answers to so many important questions that he became known as a wise person. Not all smart people become wise ones.

Because he was wise, people came from all over the world to ask Doctor Einstein questions. Many asked him easy questions, such as "How old are you?" Some asked interesting ones: "Do whales really talk to each other?" And, every now and then, someone would ask Doctor Einstein a really challenging question: "Is there life on other planets?"

One day a small person with a big name, and an even bigger curiosity, came to ask a question. Her name was Alexandra Elizabeth and what she wanted to know was different. She asked Doctor Einstein, "What is the most important question?"

Doctor Einstein thought Alexandra Elizabeth had asked a very wise question, and he told her so. He knew that questions as well as answers can be wise.

Doctor Einstein thought about Alexandra Elizabeth's question for a long time. He thought about it when he got dressed in the morning. He thought about it while he ate his peanut butter and banana sandwich for lunch. He thought about her question when he brushed his teeth. And he thought about it as he lay in bed with his sleeping cap on.

Alexandra Elizabeth had to be very patient waiting for Doctor Einstein's answer. She was more curious than she had ever been in her whole life. Many others also wondered what the famous scientist would say.

Alexandra Elizabeth knew the most important question wouldn't be the sort most people ask, such as "Will it rain tomorrow?" She was quite sure it wouldn't be "Where do babies come from?" though that certainly was important. She didn't even think it would be "Why did dinosaurs disappear from Earth?" although she was *very* curious about that. What would Doctor Einstein say?

Finally, Doctor Einstein believed he knew what the most important question was. A large crowd gathered to hear him reveal it, and Alexandra Elizabeth was right in front.

Doctor Einstein stood up. He cleared his throat. Then, in a voice that was a little too LOUD, because he was nervous, he announced the most important question: **Is the Universe a friendly place, or not?**

Then, since it *was* the most important question, in *his* opinion, Doctor Einstein suggested that each person think about his or her own answer to it. After that he sat down and looked over at Alexandra Elizabeth and smiled.

His question **Is the Universe a friendly place, or not?** puzzled many people. Even some who considered themselves smart didn't know why Doctor Einstein thought it was so important.

Alexandra Elizabeth listened to those around her. She heard someone say, "What a dumb question!" Others complained that coming to hear Doctor Einstein had been a waste of their time. Several suggested that maybe Doctor Einstein wasn't as wise as he was supposed to be. Alexandra Elizabeth just sat quietly and began to think about her own answer to the most important question.

Before she could think very long, Doctor Einstein came over to ask Alexandra Elizabeth and her father, who had traveled with her, if they would like to come to his house for lunch before they began their journey home. He said he hoped they liked peanut butter and banana sandwiches because that was all he knew how to cook.

As they ate their sandwiches on purple paper plates Doctor Einstein asked Alexandra Elizabeth if she was curious about discovering her answer to **Is the Universe a friendly place, or not.** Because her mouth was full, she just nodded enthusiastically, her eyes shining.

After lunch she thanked Doctor Einstein. She told him she was going to ask her mother to make a peanut butter and banana sandwich for her at least once a week.

On the trip home Alexandra Elizabeth had lots of time to think about the most important question. She knew she could answer it simply with a "Yes" or a "No," but she wanted to know why she felt the way she did.

Alexandra Elizabeth remembered Doctor Einstein had told her that each person carried the answer inside. She closed her eyes.

Pictures began to form in her mind. Alexandra Elizabeth saw the faces of people who looked afraid that others weren't going to be nice to them. She watched as she saw herself smile at someone new in school. An image of people shouting at each other on the sidewalk floated into her head.

Alexandra Elizabeth felt strong at the idea of being brave enough to try something new. Imagining someone mistreating a puppy made her sad. But, then, she pictured herself picking up a book for an old woman who had dropped it. She thought about how much safer she felt if her parents listened to her when she was scared.

Alexandra Elizabeth found herself thinking of the pansies in the park turning their sweet flower faces to the sky. And the sun sparkling like stars on the pond near her grandmother's house. She heard herself singing back to the birds. She remembered a time when she had so much energy that her walking just naturally turned into skipping.

Alexandra Elizabeth opened her eyes. She felt so good that she laughed out loud. Then, being a curious person, she began to wonder where laughs come from.

Inside herself, Alexandra Elizabeth knew her answer to **Is the Universe a friendly place, or not.** She realized that the way she thought created the way she felt. She began to understand why Doctor Einstein believed it was the most important question.

She wondered how others would answer the question. Would their answers change if they changed the way they thought?

Looking out the window, Alexandra Elizabeth saw a rainbow stretching across the sky. Over the rainbow was a message, a *very friendly* message. Her heart opened to receive it.

Alexandra Elizabeth had a feeling that the message was a gift from the Universe especially for her. She also knew the message was for everyone, everywhere.

Have you thought about *your* answer to
the most important question?

# POSTSCRIPTS

**Albert Einstein** (1879–1955) is widely regarded as one of the most influential people of all time. He once suggested that the most important question we can ask ourselves is: *"***Is the Universe a friendly place, or not?***"* In his opinion, how we answer this question determines our individual, and humanity's, destiny.

The colors in the illustrations of *The Most Important Question* are those that traditionally correspond to the *chakras,* or spiritual energy centers of the human body. You may have noticed that the same color scheme and order appear as rainbows and prismatic light: red, orange, yellow, green, blue, indigo, and violet. As the reader follows the story these colors are "rolled" to create patterns that carry the healing vibration of hope and promise.

**H. Constance Hill** has been an independent journalist and author since 1980. For many years she specialized in travel writing. Global journeying changed her world view from national to international. Connie's breadth of experience in the physical realm nourished her inner awareness.

Having delved deeply into metaphysics, she continues to be both student and teacher of mind/body/spirit workshops. Her artistic and communications talents combine uniquely to create healing works of art and letters.

Photo by Jean O'Neil

H. Constance Hill is also the author of *Wisdom From Beyond,* a collection of messages from 35 high profile personalities, all now returned to the spirit realm. These contributors have reached out from their perspective there to communicate profound words of guidance for those of us living on Earth now.